Where We Part

Bill McConnell

BookLeaf
Publishing

India | USA | UK

Made with ❤ on the BookLeaf Publishing Platform
www.bookleafpub.in
www.bookleafpub.com

Dedication

For the old version of me, for whom love was not
enough;
For the new version of me, for whom love is a gift.

Preface

There are moments in our lives when the space between words, the distance in familiar rooms, or the quiet absence of someone close can weigh heavier than any spoken truth. This book, a collection of poems on love, loss, and leaving, explores the hollow spaces we carry and the fragments we leave behind when we decide to walk away.

These poems are not only about endings but also the self-discovery that follows: the quiet strength in packing a suitcase, the hidden guilt of choosing peace over chaos, and the bittersweet ache of remembering tenderness alongside hurt. They trace the slow dismantling of shared lives, the reckoning with unmet needs, and the courage it takes to choose oneself over the comfort of routine.

With each verse, these pages explore the private, often unspoken moments when we realize that love, though powerful, may not always be enough to sustain us.

These poems hold space for anyone who has felt the deep pull of longing and the complex release of letting go. They are for the parts of ourselves that wonder what could have been and, eventually, come to terms with what is.

This collection invites you to journey through the ache and beauty of moving forward, one line at a time. May it offer a sense of kinship, a reminder that even in leaving, we are never truly alone.

Acknowledgements

These poems are born from personal experiences that have shaped, challenged, and ultimately transformed me. Each line is a reflection of the moments I lived, the choices I made, and the realizations that came to light through leaving, longing, and learning to let go. Writing these poems has been a way to make sense of the complex landscape of love and loss—a journey that, while intensely personal, resonates with the shared experience of finding strength within vulnerability.

I am grateful for the lessons embedded in every memory, every difficult decision, and every quiet reflection that became part of this collection. To the parts of myself that grew, even when growth was painful, and to the courage it took to embrace clarity over comfort—thank you.

These words are, in their way, a testament to resilience, and I honor the journey that inspired them. Thank you for being part of this process.

ONE. What do you want to know?

You said i don't
Really know you.

What do you want to know?

That I drink my coffee black so that my
Day is the bitterest in the morning,
so I have more room
for joy in the afternoons?

Or that plucking my eyebrows makes me sneeze
for twenty minutes, cursing God
for every hair, each soul-thread rips away?

Or that on really hot days,
after spending time
in an icebox-of-an-air-conditioned room --
Transmuting into freeze-dried jerky --
I like to go sit in my car, where the thermostat reads
One-hundred-twelve degrees Fahrenheit,
And feel my skin prickle with goosebumps,
And watch the arm hairs bolt up so suddenly
that I feel sick with the heat and blood

coursing through the webs of spider veins
along my limbs and neck.

Or that when I love, I bruise myself deeply,
Taking in too much at once,
Offering up too much in return,
probably too quickly --

(My heart is made of glass, you know)

--yet again.

Or that my passion surges,
as fierce as drink, like every kiss
is something I could drown in.

I look at the symmetry of your face,
see each tender, human flaw—
the slant of your smile, your left brow
just slightly thinner, the almond tilt
of your right eye—my memory holds you,
each detail, like a snowflake, one of a kind.

I listen when you speak
of needing water by the bed,
a fan in the heat, red wine sulfite-free
to soothe your midnight heartburn.

I listen when you tell me to move closer,
glide a hand across your skin,
drawing a soft moan from the shadows.
And you arch, whispering,
"It's like you know me."

To me, you feel like home.

So is it fear when you say,
"I don't really know you?"

What do you want to know?

That I drink my coffee black so that my
day is bitterest at dawn,
leaving more room for joy
to filter in?
Or that I end my nights with whiskey,
toasting the unknown—
a quiet ache for home.

2. How we met

We met at a conference.
Sitting at the bar, scanning the crowd—
laughter like drunken hyenas,
their noise grating my nerves.

Across from me, a very drunk woman
smiled through her whiskey, slurring,
"You're hot," her glass a smudged halo.

Then you walked up, wine in hand,
holding it close, your security blanket,
murmuring to yourself.

I leaned in, capturing each word
like a tape recorder on stealth mode.
"I do love my husband. I do,"
you whispered, a rosary chant to
Saint Goretti, or maybe Saint Valentine.

The noise swelled. The drunk woman kept up
her praise, calling me "hot," though the only heat
was the burn on my neck, under my collar.

An orphaned plate of nachos appeared,

and I claimed it, moved to a quiet table
behind me, hoping for silence.

I offered to share. You shared your wine.
Your smile drew me in. We talked of our mothers—
both lost to cancer. Trauma bonding, but bonding still.

More wine. The bar closed. We bought a cheap red
from the hotel store, found a table in a dark corner.
The crowd gone, we were alone.

My hand found your knee. You leaned in,
and we kissed. "Let's go upstairs."

In the elevator, lips and hands roamed,
reaching, desperate, like starving
souls who hadn't seen fresh bread in weeks.

In my room, we opened the bottle,
you slipped to the bathroom. Naked on the bed,
I fell asleep to the door's soft click,
as you ran into the hallway's safety,
innocence intact, though intent less pure—
Saint Maria Goretti, your silent witness.

3. Priorities

She argued with me
about priorities, about how
she hoped I'd choose
to spend my time
as her time.

And all I could
say was, *"You're right.*
You do come first.
Your wants.
Your needs.
First."

What I wanted,
didn't matter.
What I worked for,
didn't matter.
What I needed—
faded in silence.

I need connection,
to feel deeply,
to desire and be desired—
to be touched,

your fingers sharp against
the skin of my back.

But you weren't listening.

Did you know my
love language is touch?
And my other is the sharing of dreams,
so that as we sail this boat together,
we won't be pulled apart,
shredded in storms
that tear us through opposing tides.

But you weren't listening.

So I walked away,
because no one is harder
to love than someone
who cannot meet me halfway.

4. Her Scent

What do I remember
about you?

Your smell, like lavender
on a cool fall breeze,

or as a hot tea
steeped with cinnamon,
honey, lemon—

not too sweet or bitter,
a blend of personality.

There's a musky tinge,
like after sex,
floral and dark,
unique to your skin.

I leave the sheets unwashed
after you've spent the night,
just to breathe you in
a day or two more,
letting your memory linger awhile longer.

5. The morning after

The next morning,
I apologized to you—

after all, we're both married,
both involved, both vowed
until death do us part.

You told me not to apologize,
said you didn't regret a thing.

"We're just two right people
at the wrong time," you said,
"in some other timeline,
this would be right."

At Figueroa and 4th, outside the Bonaventure,
I watched you cross the street,
enter the parking garage,
and return to the life
where you "love your husband."

At home, I wore a face like a mask
for what happened,
and for what didn't.

I used to wonder how men
who cheat could go home,
look their wives in the eye,
and act like it was nothing.

I think I know now.

Little boxes in the mind—
one for her, one for the wife—
where each lives apart, untouched,
compartmentalized, each only lights
one at a time.

It makes me sick, even now,
to think of switching between the two.

they flicker on and off, like a light switch,
my fingers careful not to spark fire.

6. Time

I don't know when the right time will be
For you and me,
For our hearts to beat in sync,
For our breaths to mingle in our heat,
For our bodies to share a space
Built on connection.

For us to look back on the years and wonder--
How we ever lived without the other.

15. Anxiety, Confusion, and Apprehension, in that order.

#1: Anxiety
Tonight, my heart can hardly catch its breath;
A panic sets my world in disarray.
The thought of losing you feels like a death,
But still, I push you from my heart's own fray.
For love has hurt me, left me in the dust,
Each promise shattered, trust reduced to ash.
And though I crave to give in, to be just,
I fear that I'll repeat the same old crash.
Yet still, I love the quiet peace we find
When laughter fills the garden air with light.
Your presence offers solace to my mind,
But fear of time's betrayal keeps me tight.
I sip this wine; it's bitter to the core,
And in its taste, I doubt just a bit more.

#2: Confusion
I don't know why we met in this strange hour,
A tangle of confusion, love, and chance.
Your presence stirs a dormant, quiet power,
But timing stands between us like a lance.

The way you touch my hand, it calms my soul;
I crave the peace you offer with your eyes.
But broken men have left me far from whole,
Their fleeting passion full of empty lies.
I wish that fate had brought you to my door
When I was brave enough to trust again.
But caution reigns; I fear what lies in store,
Afraid to break, yet bound to you in pain.
The world has brought us here in shades of gray,
But could we flourish in some brighter day?

#3: Apprehension
Time trudges on; it never waits for me,
Nor grants the space to see what I will do.
Impatience churns in moments I can't flee,
And in my heart, these fears are born anew.
You're not escape, not boredom in disguise,
Yet here I stand uncertain, locked in doubt.
I feel the weight of all my past goodbyes,
Afraid of hurt, unsure what love's about.
I see you through the lens of what could be,
Yet time itself obscures the clearest view.
I want to leap, to set my worries free,
But scars remind me of what I once knew.
So now I stand, a soul too scared to soar,
Wondering if love's worth fighting for.

8. Covid Check

A week later, your email appeared—
"How are you feeling?" you asked.
*"I found your email from the group.
I hope it's okay I'm reaching out."*

I thought back to the hotel room:
me, naked under the sheets,
you standing by the bed, whispering,
"We can't do this," before you slipped
out the door.

I should have run after you,
drunk, wrapped in a sheet
like Caesar claiming lands beyond Rome,
places I had no right to rule.

But I lay still, relieved at your exit,
yet reeling, wondering what lines
I'd been willing to cross.

The next morning, I apologized.
You smiled. *"I'm not sorry.
I wanted to. I would have."*

"Sit with me," you said,
and we spent the day
mostly in silence, sharing
a few words, but avoiding
what almost was.

So I wrote back: *I'm confused,*
overwhelmed by you—hating
that I apologized, loving your lack
of regret. Coffee? Tea?
Maybe we could talk.

You replied almost instantly—
Silly, I have Covid. I meant
are you sick? Are you feeling okay?

Then a second email,
two minutes later:
But maybe meeting could help—
to pull back clouds and reveal green fields
where dust and stone reside,
to find streams and rivers
in the dry bed of tumbleweeds,
to reveal hope,
where there's only disappointment.

And now, I ask back—
Are you feeling okay?

16

9. Seeing Clearly

A year before I met you,
I told my wife I wanted LASIK—
wanted to see the world
for once without glasses.

Earliest memories: sitting in Dr. Robson's office,
Ontario winters fogging the windows,
staring at cartoon characters, deciding—
version 1 or version 2? Option A or B?
Then to the fitting room,
trying on frames, my world still blurry.

The day of surgery: half a milligram of Xanax
for nerves. Who could blame me?
They show it all, real-time on a screen—
the doctor peeling back skin,
sculpting corneal flaps,
the laser tracing across my eye.

In the dark, I lose vision.
Total blindness,
not blurriness or nearsightedness—
just nothingness.
Losing sight of what's important,

or maybe for the first time
seeing what doesn't matter.

A smell like burning hair or nails—
the laser cuts its way through.
In darkness, tendrils of smoke curl,
and three figures of light dance.
One green between two red,
seducing in slow pirouettes,
like beauty tracing a path across
new eyes, pixelating onto my cornea.

The scent brings back
childhood crimes—murdering ants,
sometimes beetles, with a magnifying glass.
Morbid curiosity,
a sadness at choosing destruction.

Now I hold your hand,
sitting with you on a bench,
seeing clearly the almond tilt of your eyes.
And I think of that glass again,
that lens that once burned,
is now destroying a life (perhaps two)
but not out of curiosity—
no, I knew exactly what I chose.

With you, I find calm,
a serene focus, my desires clarified,
clear yet selfish.

You ask the questions—
What are we doing?
What do we want from each other?
Can this ever work?

The doctor once asked the same
about my eyes; there was a time
when my vision was beyond repair,
when the tools simply couldn't fix it.

But technology advanced,
the procedure found a way,
and I think maybe time has answers,
though they might not be
the ones we want to see.

10. Done

If anyone ever tells you
that leaving is easy,
they've never waited for
a spouse to go to work,
to pack two suitcases
with the leftover scraps
from a time
before marriage.

Nor have they emptied
the medicine cabinet—
bottles with names like Ezetimibe,
Amlodipine, and Terazosine.

Nor have they said goodbye
to the best boy in the world,
the Golden Retriever,
whose whole life's work
is waiting for walks,
snacks, and belly rubs.

Nor have they sat
in their favorite chair,
one last time, feeling

the dips and sinks, the scars
left by elbows and hips.

Nor have they looked
out the back window
at the mountain view,
at the branch where the barn owl
waits to steal koi
from the backyard pond.

Nor have they lain
on the backyard dirt,
watching fifty-foot pines sway
in slow, metronomic time
with the earth's steady beat.

Nor have they driven to work
knowing they aren't coming back,
even when the phone rings
and she asks, *Are you really gone?*
And you tell her—*yes,*

done with the fighting,
done with years of
You don't make me happy,

done with trying to be

the husband you thought
you should be.

Done with her negative talk,
her constant complaints
that have rendered her
utterly unfuckable.

Done knowing
your love was never
going to be enough.

Done feeling disconnected,
treated like a roommate,
blamed for her unhappiness—
as if happiness were yours to give,
rather than something
we each learn to grow.

Done with a person
who doesn't dare to dream,
to imagine a future,
to want more, to feel more.
A simple word—
done.

11. Breaking No Contact

I kept a strict policy: no contact.
They say distance helps you see—
what you're missing or what's best left behind.

It didn't take long
to feel that peace, that quiet,
monumentally more valuable
than reuniting with chaos.

Two months went by
without a phone call.

Then, on a Friday in June,
my wife called.
First words out of her mouth:
"So, I guess we're getting a divorce."

Not a question.

I didn't bother to tell her
I'd already hired a lawyer.

Secretly, I was hoping she'd
softened somehow,

that two months apart
might have worn away her edges.

It wasn't too late.
It's never too late.

But before I could say this,
she laid out my wrongs—
all the things I'd said
too hurtful, too spiteful
to take back.

So I replied, "I'll hire an attorney,
start the process. You should get one, too."

She said she couldn't afford one.

We talked division—
what "half" would look like.
She was thinking more like six divided by two,
or eight divided by one.

I told her again: get an attorney.

Before I hung up, I told her,
I should have been more like Icarus,
and soared closer to the sun.

Better to burn in the heat,
chasing stars,
than to waste a life fearing
the pull of a furious sea.

12. What I Said: Part 1

We talk in circles, anger all around,
Yet silence seals what's breaking us apart.
Our words fall heavy, never touching ground.

You say you're lonely, love's touch not profound,
While guilt and distance nestle in my heart—
We talk in circles, anger all around.

Each promise withers, actions unrenowned,
Attempts to bridge the gulf a clumsy start,
Our words fall heavy, never touching ground.

To be two strangers in a bond unbound,
The weight we bear as every vow departs—
We talk in circles, anger all around.

I say I'll try to be the man you found,
Yet find myself withdrawn, as shadows dart.
Our words fall heavy, never touching ground.

So round we go, familiar as the sound—
In silence bound, two souls that drift apart.
We talk in circles, anger all around;
Our words fall heavy, never touching ground.

13. What I Said: Part 2

Each day is filled with words that speak of little—
The aches of work, complaints of daily strain.
But silence breeds the heartache that we nurture,
Where loneliness has wound its roots in deep,
And joy feels like a language long forgotten,
Two strangers in a life we built by name.

For fourteen years, we tried to make a name,
But knowing "us" or "we" means almost little,
When in our space, our dreams are long forgotten,
And every conversation, stale and strained.
We rarely pause to ask what lies so deep,
In hearts where disconnected paths now nurture.

What once was warmth, the years of love did nurture,
Has faded into roles that lack their name,
And words unspoken now are buried deep.
How did we let this life become so little,
That even in each other's arms we strain,
As if our memories themselves forgotten?

It's sad to think our love has been forgotten,
To see what we have come to break and nurture—
Two hollowed lives where once we never strained

To feel the depth of what we'd grown in name,
Yet now, it feels like holding onto little,
Pretending joy that neither of us feel deep.

And maybe it's the space we need, so deep
We'll find what once in wonder was forgotten,
Unearth a way beyond what feels so little.
We'll tend our own hearts in the time we nurture,
To look within and find a truer name,
Apart, no longer caught in endless strain.

If freedom means we live beyond this strain,
Perhaps we'll mend what's broken far too deep.
Perhaps it means we seek another name,
And let what's past be tenderly forgotten,
And from a space that solitude might nurture,
Find joy beyond what binds us now to little.

14. What I Said: Part 3

I don't think I am the man for you,
These last fights have left me hollowed out.
In silence and in anger, we pull through,
But happiness feels like a distant doubt.

These last fights have left me hollowed out—
The weight of words grows heavy day by day,
And happiness feels like a distant doubt.
Perhaps in leaving, we find our own way.

The weight of words grows heavy day by day;
Two strangers, in a house that feels undone.
Perhaps in leaving, we find our own way—
To heal, and know ourselves as we begun.

Two strangers, in a house that feels undone,
In silence and in anger, we pull through.
To heal, and know ourselves as we begun—
I don't think I am the man for you.

15. Assets and Wage

Marriage amounts to lines on a page,
Just numbers filling columns and rows.
Our lives are reduced to assets and wage.

Divorce lawyer asks what I'd exchange,
A ledger now marking the highs and lows—
Marriage amounts to lines on a page.

My work and laughter, both neatly caged,
Work and friends now marked as mere prose—
Marriage amounts to lines on a page.

Old Man Dave, with his stories aged,
No place in the ledger where his value shows.
Our lives are reduced to assets and wage.

Or making soap with a gentle rage,
Pushing my craft, yet no worth it bestows—
Marriage amounts to lines on a page.

Or late weeknights, while discussions raged,
Songs strummed, guitar warmed in firelight's glow.
Our lives are reduced to assets and wage.

But people, they say, are mere loss and gauge,
Cold numbers that tick and balance and close.
Marriage amounts to lines on a page;
Our lives are reduced to assets and wage.

16. Side by Side

The first time we lay side by side,
After I'd left, no strings to hold.
You poured cheap wine over watermelon,
Turning red cabernet into gold.

After I'd left, no strings to hold,
You booked us a room at the Mission Inn,
Turning red cabernet into gold,
Sugary drops slipping, sweet and bold.

You booked us a room at the Mission Inn—
We laughed, we drank, we slipped outside,
Sugary drops slipping, sweet and bold,
Karaoke songs, mushrooms shifting the light.

We laughed, we drank, we slipped outside,
Held hands steady, climbed up the stairs.
Karaoke songs, mushrooms shifting the light,
Legs carrying us to that waiting bed.

Held hands steady, climbed up the stairs,
Your mouth on mine, a kiss to consume,
Legs carrying us to that waiting bed,
Licking my teeth, my honesty fading.

Your mouth on mine, a kiss to consume,
You poured cheap wine over watermelon,
Licking my teeth, my honesty fading—
The first time we lay side by side.

17. A Short Break

In June, the month of warmth and sweet rebirth,
I never thought new life would come to me.
You pulled into my space and said, *we need
to speak of things that weigh upon my heart.*

My stomach turned; I felt a sudden dread—
the kind that rises fast and sharp and sure.
I feared you'd tell me I was losing you,
a rush of heat and sickness filled my chest.

I'd brought three gifts for you, so small, but still,
a tuner, strings, and some oil for the wood.
You'd bought a Songbird; I prepared its home,
to keep its body whole, uncracked, and strong.

And isn't it the same with love and flesh?
A woman, like a guitar, needs such care:
you moisturize and keep her parts in tune,
you pluck the strings and listen to her hum.

You tried to mend the past returning to him,
though not quite *ex*, not truly gone away—
two rooms, two beds, but still the house is shared,
with walls and silence built of guilt and space.

Is it your faith that draws you back to him,
to him, whose family pulls you far from here?
You traveled far; I messaged you that song,
the Cranberries' tune you couldn't seem to play.

I sent my heart, a sink that will not drain—
not like your faucet shutting off at once.
The rivers of your heart so dry and still,
While the waters of mine cause me to drown

I didn't think that I would hear from you,
unless it came in anger, sharp and cold.
But you returned to me, not lost, but found,
ran back into my arms, to love be bound

18. In the Botanical Gardens

Sitting in the shade of leaves, your hand reaches for
mine,
in quiet gardens waiting, where our moments intertwine.
You bring a basket weighed with wine and summer's
taste,
with cheese and laughter, we rest under petals' shine.

Beneath a sun that clings like sweetness on our skin,
you thought of my hunger, offered me a lifeline.
A tray filled with treats, simple yet rich with care,
fruit and fresh bread laid out, with olives in a line.

For all the tender ways you thought to nourish me,
I find myself bound, drawn to you like tangled vine.

19. Date Night in the Vegas Heat

It must be 117 degrees outside, not *a*
moment of relief in the Las Vegas sun, no rose
petals on the pavement, only heat radiating by.
We walk, faces scrunched like paper, any
slight breeze would be mercy; another other
sweltering afternoon burns through sunscreen, name
brands don't matter when the sun strikes this hard, would
we make it through the crossing, blistered feet that smell
of scorched rubber soles. But the lobby's air, cold as
an icebox, pulls us in with a blast of cool relief, sweet.

20. Start Over

At fifty-two, starting over isn't easy,
To leave a home, a wife, a life behind.
Some might think I'm blind or crazy—
At fifty-two, starting over isn't easy.

Chasing the sun like a young man, breezy,
While my heart's grown tired but my mind's unkind.
At fifty-two, starting over isn't easy,
To leave a home, a wife, a life behind.

Leaving behind a home, a wife, a life,
At fifty-two, starting over isn't easy.
Some call it foolish, or maybe even crazy—
Leaving behind a home, a wife, a life.

I chase the sun and flirt with strife,
A young man's heart in a body uneasy.
Leaving behind a home, a wife, a life,
At fifty-two, starting over isn't easy.

At fifty-two, starting over isn't easy,
Leaving behind a home, a wife, a life.
Some call it foolish, or maybe even crazy—
At fifty-two, starting over isn't easy.

Chasing dreams in the light, though my heart feels hazy,
Still flirting with time, through age and strife.
At fifty-two, starting over isn't easy,
Leaving behind a home, a wife, a life.

21. When I Tell You I Miss You

When I tell you I miss you, how
I miss the space you leave, the scent of your lavender I
find clinging in the air on the morning breeze, which
makes me wish
for that silence we shared. You, turning thoughts, you
never spoke, but your presence was enough—just were.

When I tell you I miss you here,
it's your laugh I miss, the way we're
two beats of music, bodies lost
in movement, your hips pulsing like souls
leaping through light. Dancing, laughing, living
in rhythms that hold the world close in
every cruelty and beauty, trapped like a
secret kept safe within walls, as fragile as a fish
breathing shallow. I count time in this bowl

until I'm dreaming of you, night after
night, a memory I cradle each year
more deeply, lying awake and running
your words in my mind, tracing them over
like footsteps that wander the same

path we walked, your touch a spark, old
but never tired, never worn. I cover this ground

41

with you in my thoughts, wondering how
I'd tell you I miss you, yet we found
the gentlest way to stay, but fear
that all I hold dear is just a wish,
a hope to feel you, to know you were
by my side, waiting to come home, here.